All-In-One
Piano Lessons

Book D

Authors
Barbara Kreader, Fred Kern,
Phillip Keveren, Mona Rejino

Consultants
Tony Caramia, Bruce Berr,
Richard Rejino

Manager, Educational Piano
Jennifer Linn

Editor
Anne Wester

Illustrator
Fred Bell

To access audio visit:
www.halleonard.com/mylibrary

Enter Code
3429-8024-3891-9069

FOREWORD

Building on the success of the **All-In-One Piano Lessons Books A** and **B**, the **All-In-One Piano Lessons Books C** and **D** combine selected pages from the original Level 2 Piano Lessons, Technique, Solos, Theory Workbook, and Practice Games into one easy-to-manage book. Upon completion of the **All-In-One Piano Lessons Books C** and **D**, students will be ready to continue into Level 3 of the **Hal Leonard Student Piano Library.**

When music excites our interest and imagination, we eagerly put our hearts into learning it. The music in the **Hal Leonard Student Piano Library** encourages practice, progress, confidence, and best of all – success! Over 1,000 students and teachers in a nationwide test market responded with enthusiasm to the:

- variety of styles and moods
- natural rhythmic flow, singable melodies and lyrics
- "best ever" teacher accompaniments
- improvisations integrated throughout the **Lesson Books**
- orchestrated accompaniments included in audio and MIDI formats.

When new concepts have an immediate application to the music, the effort it takes to learn these skills seems worth it. Test market teachers and students were especially excited about the:

- "realistic" pacing that challenges without overwhelming
- clear and concise presentation of concepts that allows room for a teacher's individual approach
- uncluttered page layout that keeps the focus on the music.

The **Hal Leonard Student Piano Library** is the result of the efforts of many individuals. We extend our gratitude to all the teachers, students and colleagues who shared their energy and creative input. May this method guide your learning as you bring this music to life.

Best wishes,

ISBN 978-1-61780-691-9

HAL•LEONARD®
CORPORATION

7777 W. BLUEMOUND RD. P.O. BOX 13819 MILWAUKEE, WI 53213

Visit Hal Leonard Online at
www.halleonard.com

CONTENTS

Sharps

1. Trace the sharps below.

space sharp   **line sharp**

2. Draw a sharp sign in the box before each note.
3. Write the name of each note in the blank below it.

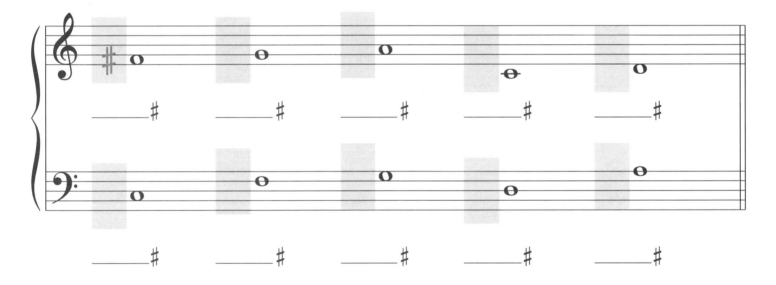

4. Write the name of the sharp key in the blank above each key.

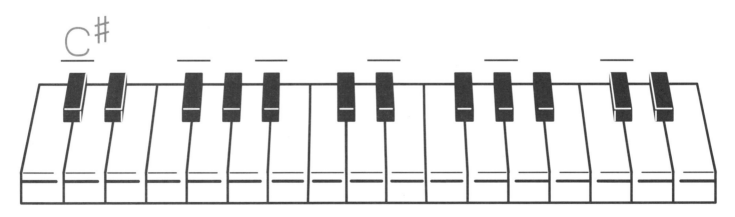

4

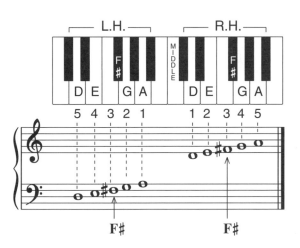

Little River Flowing

Folk Tune

Smoothly

Accompaniment (Student plays one octave higher than written.) 🔊 1/2

Smoothly (♩=145)

With pedal

Quiet Thoughts

H. Berens
(1826–1880)
Op. 62
Adapted by Fred Kern

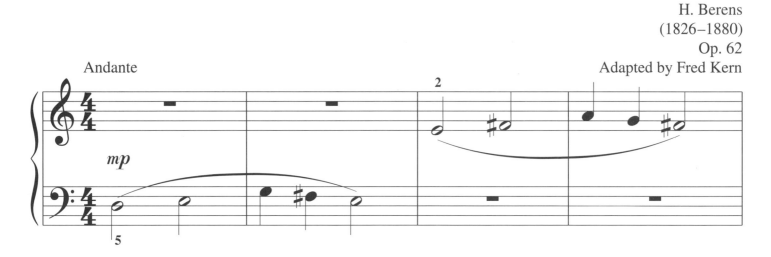

When a sharp appears before a note,
it remains sharp for one entire measure.

Accompaniment (Student plays one octave higher than written.) 🔊 3/4

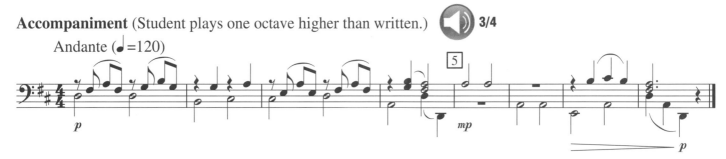

Quiet Thoughts
(Activity Page)

1. Play this version of *Quiet Thoughts* without the sharps
   (using the white keys only).

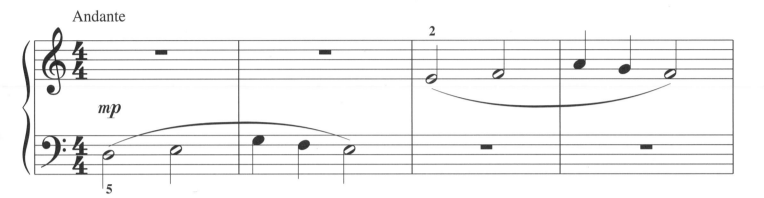

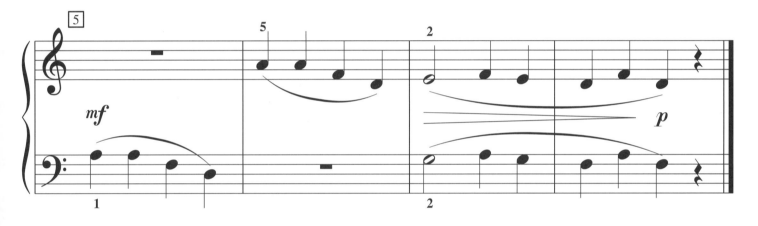

2. Practice writing a sharp in front of each note below.

Line-note sharps
(line cuts through the center of the ♯)

Space-note sharps
(center of ♯ fills the space)

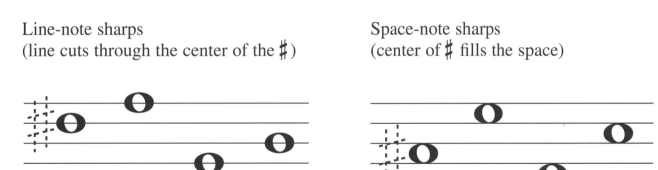

3. Add the missing sharps to the score of *Quiet Thoughts* above, using your lesson book as
   a guide.

4. To find out if you added all the sharps correctly, play your score of *Quiet Thoughts* to see
   if it sounds the same as the version on page 6.

Handbells

Ringing

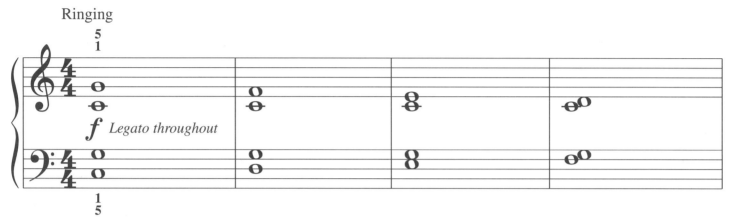

f *Legato throughout*

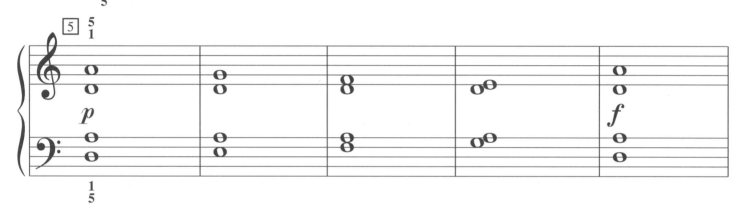

p

f

ff

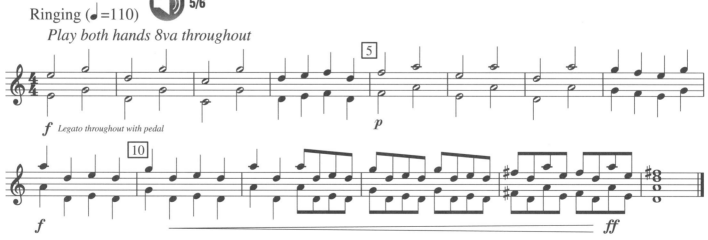

Accompaniment

Ringing (♩=110) 5/6

Play both hands 8va throughout

f *Legato throughout with pedal*

p

f

ff

8

A-Rest

Accompaniment (Student plays one octave higher than written.) 🔊 7/8

The Accompaniment

Student Accompaniment

With energy

Bill Boyd

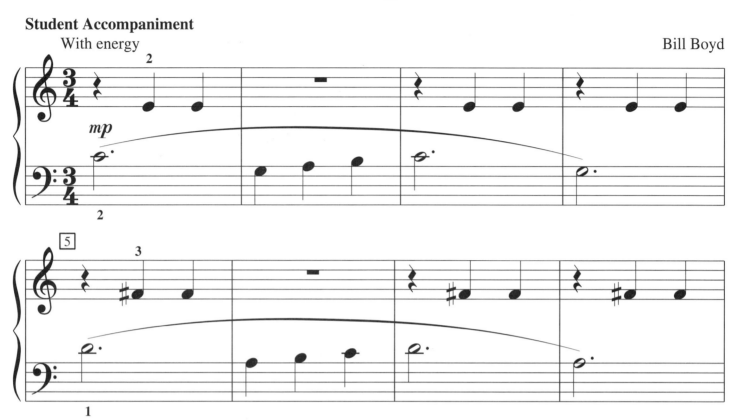

A sharp before a note lasts for only one measure.

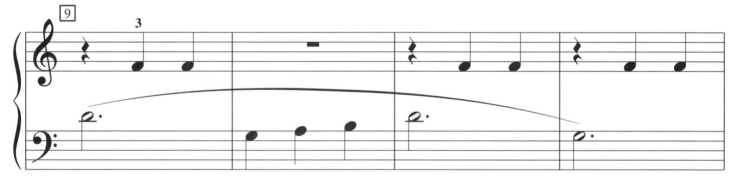

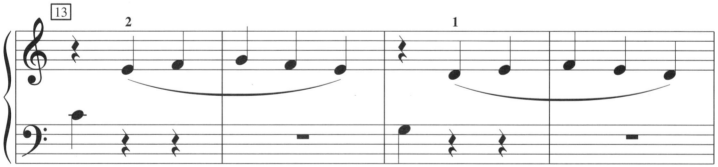

Teacher Solo (Student plays one octave lower than written. Teacher may play one octave higher than written.)

With energy ($\quarternote$ = 175) **9/10**

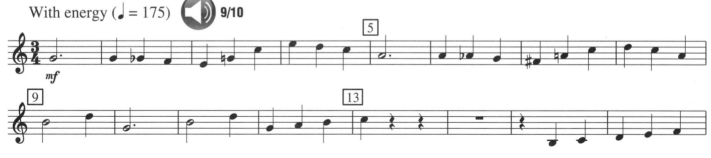

10

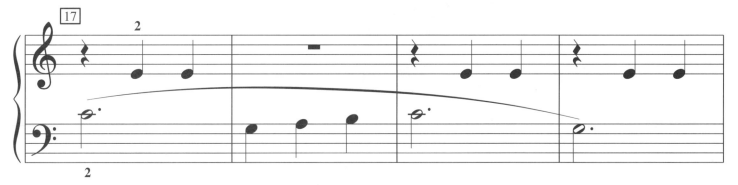

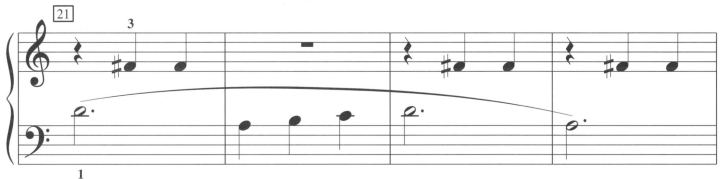

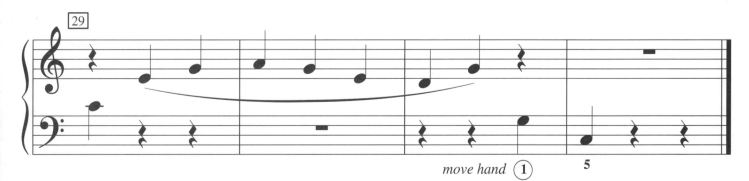

move hand ① 5

Tribal Celebration

Christos Tsitsaros

Accompaniment (Student plays one octave higher than written.) 🔊 **11/12**

Medium fast ($\quad$ = 200)

mp drum-like

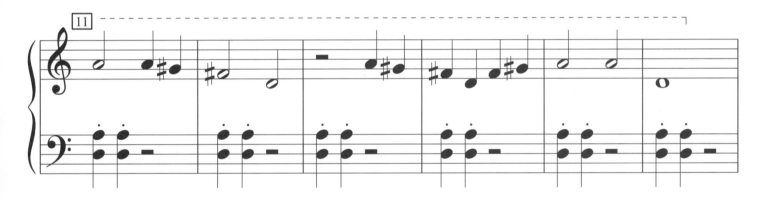

* When the sign *loco* appears, play the notes where written.

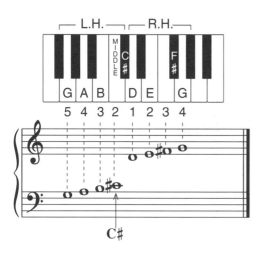

Star Quest

Phillip Keveren

A

Heroic March

f Glid - ing through the heav - ens, won - der where we are?

Great ga - lac - tic trav - 'lers, search - ing for a star.

Fine

Accompaniment (Student plays one octave higher than written.) 🔊 **13/14**

Heroic March (♩=120)

B

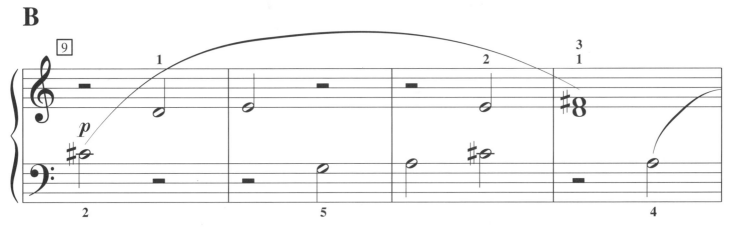

D.C. al Fine

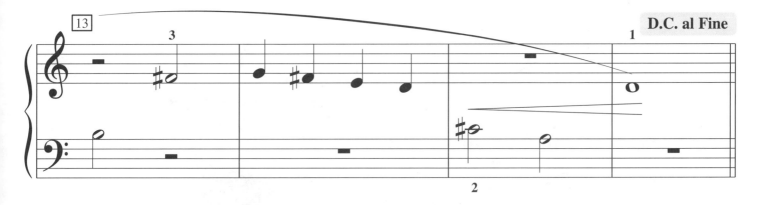

Listening To Form –
Is It A Or B?

Bear will show you how sections
of music fit together by using his **A** and **B** balloons.

The **A Section** is the
main theme of the piece.

The **B Section** is a
different but related theme.

Color this **A** balloon red.

Color this **B** balloon blue.

1. As you listen to your teacher play each piece, identify the **A** and **B** sections.
2. As you listen a second time, your teacher will play only the **A Section** or only the **B Section** of each piece. Color the balloons that match the sections you hear.

Twinkle Twinkle Little Star

Pierrot

Old MacDonald Had A Farm

Teacher's Examples on pg. 71

Meditation

Peacefully

Accompaniment (Student plays one octave higher than written.) 🔊 **15/16**

Peacefully (♩=95)

Take It Slow

Slowly (♩ = 85)

Bill Boyd

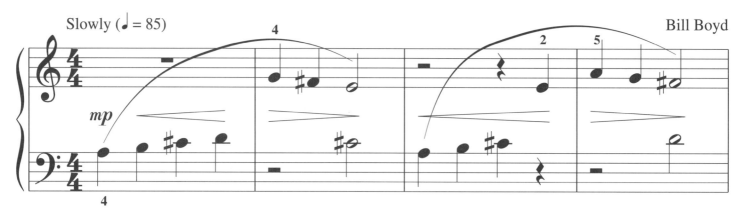

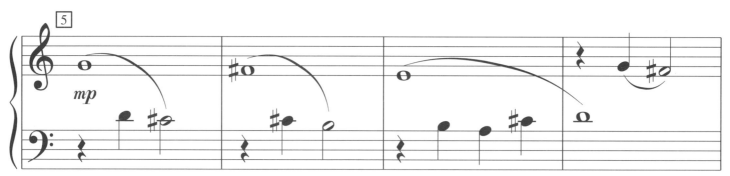

Accompaniment (Student plays one octave higher than written.) 🔊 **17/18**

Slowly (♩ = 85)

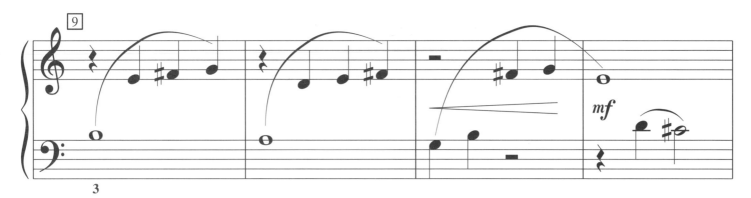

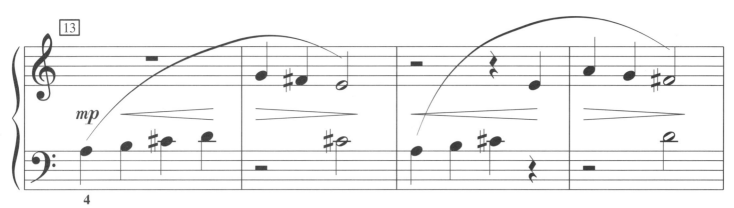

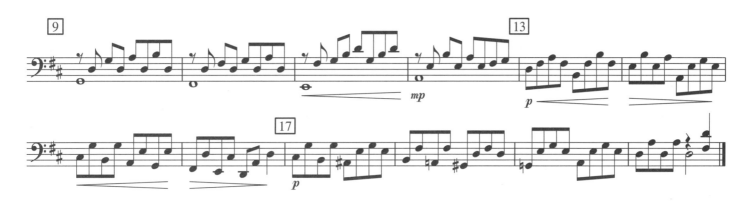

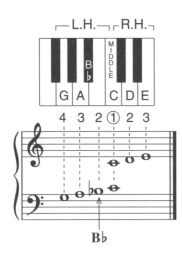

A Little Latin

Moderately fast

Bill Boyd

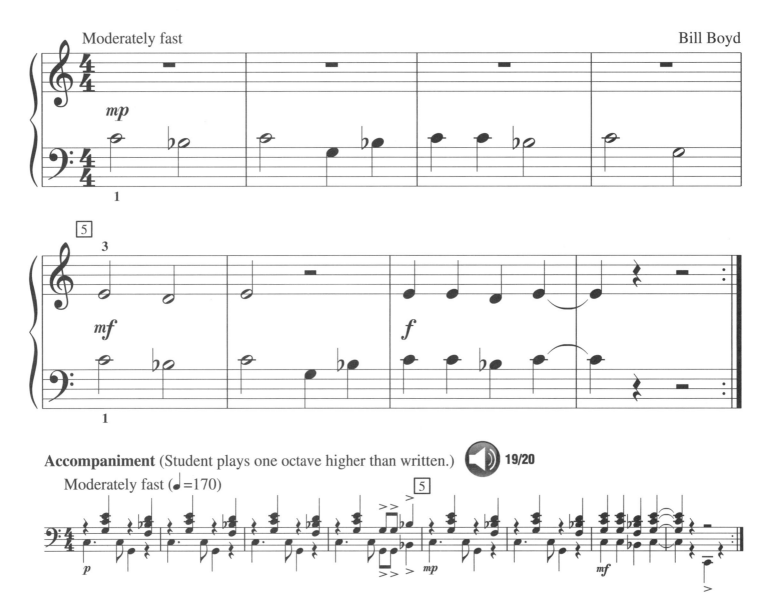

Accompaniment (Student plays one octave higher than written.) 19/20

Moderately fast (♩=170)

Flats

1. Trace the flats below.

space flat

line flat

2. Draw a flat sign in the box before each note.
3. Write the name of each note in the blank below it.

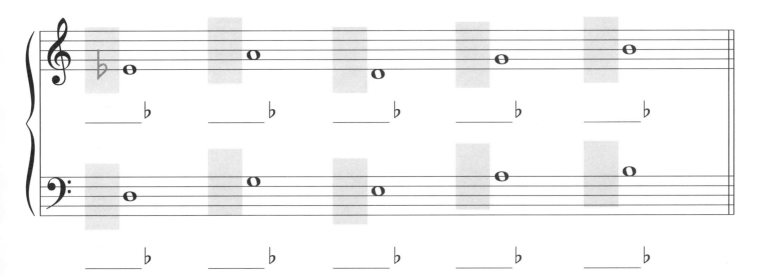

4. Write the name of the flat key in the blank above each key.

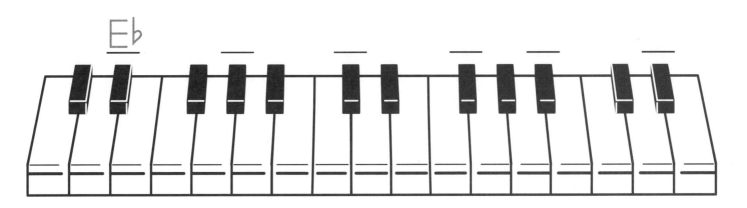

A Little Latin

(Activity Page)

1. *A Little Latin* loses some of its appeal when you play it without the B♭ in the L.H. Play this version of *A Little Latin* without the flats (using the white keys only).

Moderately fast

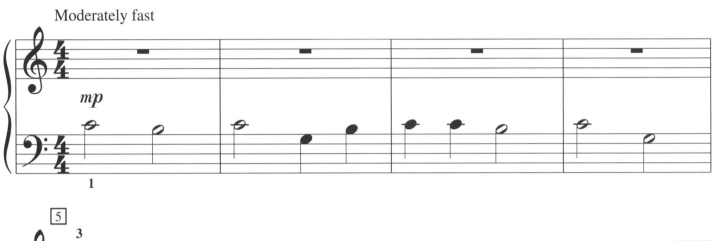

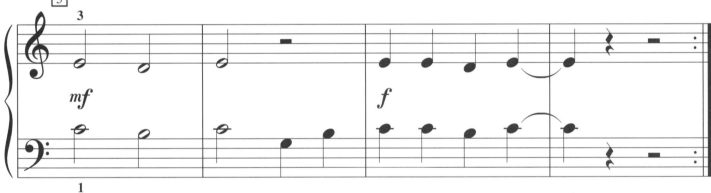

2. Practice writing a flat in front of each note below.

Line-note flats
(line cuts through the ♭)

Space-note flats
(♭ fills the space)

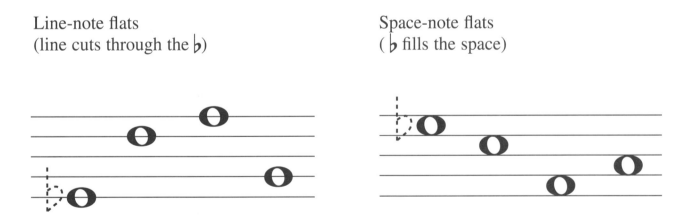

3. Add the missing flats to the score of *A Little Latin* above, using your lesson book as a guide.

4. To find out if you added all the flats correctly, play your score of *A Little Latin* to see if it sounds the same as the version in your lesson book.

A Little Latin
(Improv Activity)

 19/20

Let your hands talk to each other!

One way to create a piece is to trade phrases between your hands, playing first one hand and then the other. Make up your own piece using the following notes in both hands:

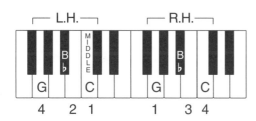

1. As you listen to the accompaniment to *A Little Latin*, play along as your R.H. asks a musical question and your L.H. answers back.

2. As your teacher plays the 12-bar blues accompaniment below, make up your own melody using the same notes in question and answer phrases between the hands.

Teacher Accompaniment
Moderately fast (♩ = 170)

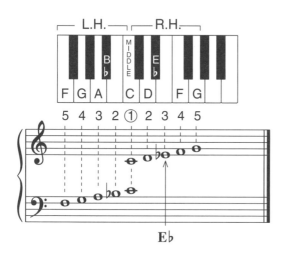

Eb

Stompin'

Keep the beat! (♩=190) 🔊 **21/22**

Bill Boyd

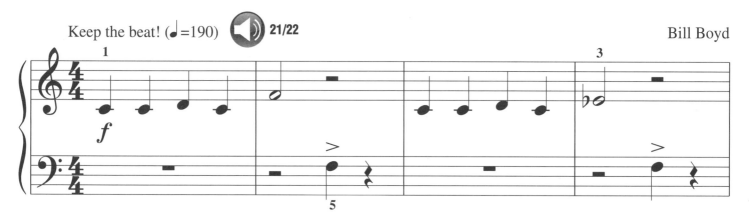

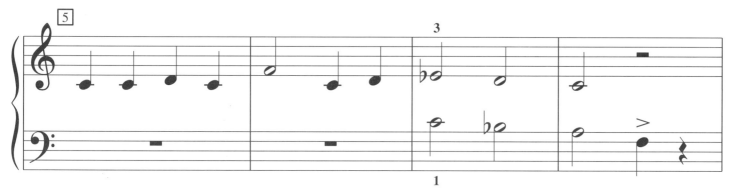

D♯ is the same piano key as E♭.

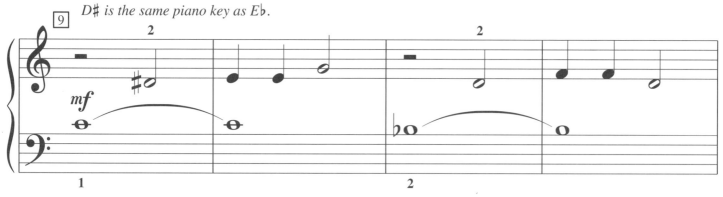

24

Stompin'
(Improv Activity)

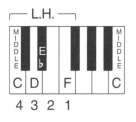

Get ready to improvise!

1. In jazz style, a repeated accompaniment pattern is called a **vamp**. Practice playing the L.H. vamp below.

Repeat as necessary

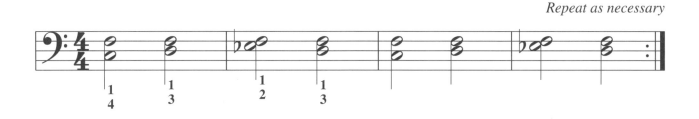

2. When you can play the L.H. vamp easily, use it as an introduction to your improvisation. Keep the vamp going as you improvise a melody in your R.H. using notes C D E♭ F.

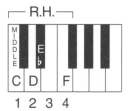

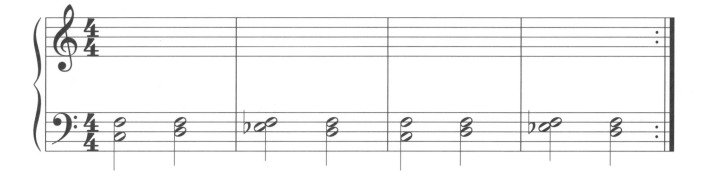

3. When you are ready to complete your improvisation, add the following ending:

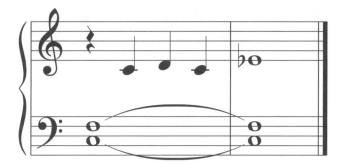

Viva La Rhumba!

Allegro

Carol Klose

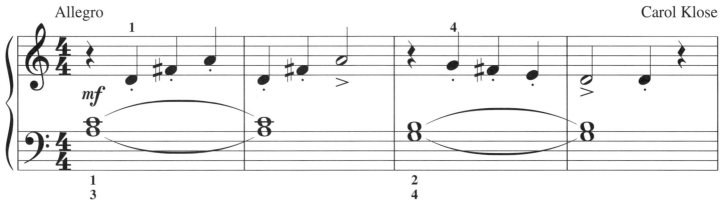

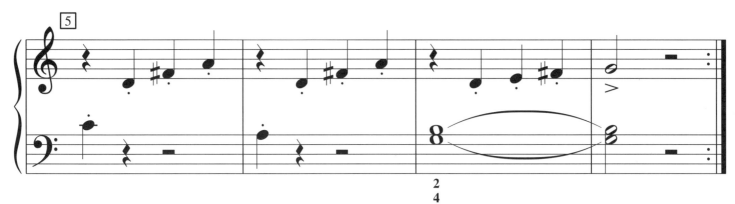

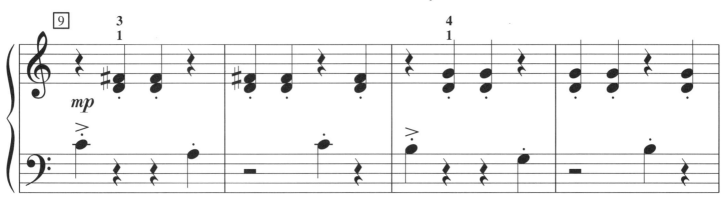

Accompaniment (Student plays one octave higher than written.) 🔊 **23/24**

Allegro (♩ = 120)

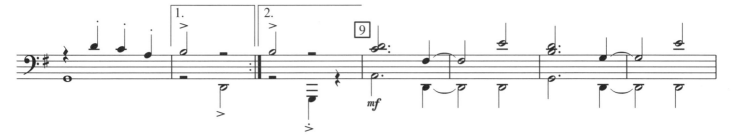

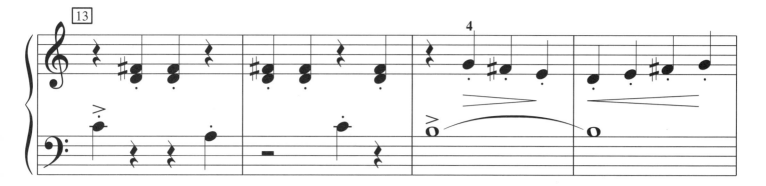

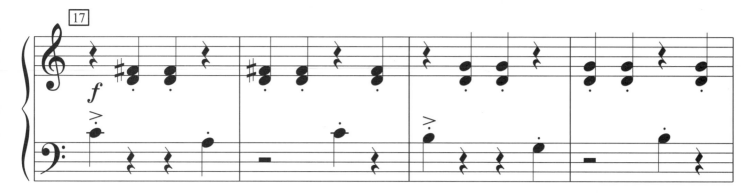

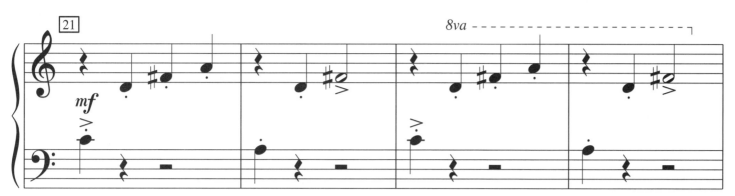

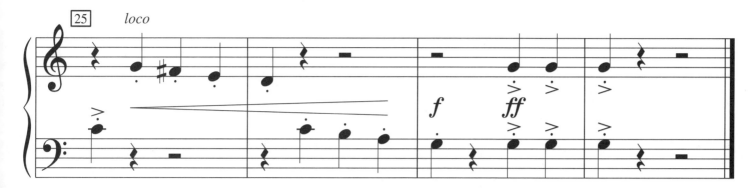

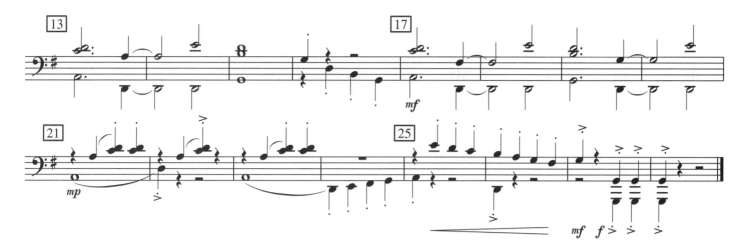

RITARD

Ritard or *rit.* means to slow the tempo gradually.

First Light

Gaelic Melody
Words by Fred Kern

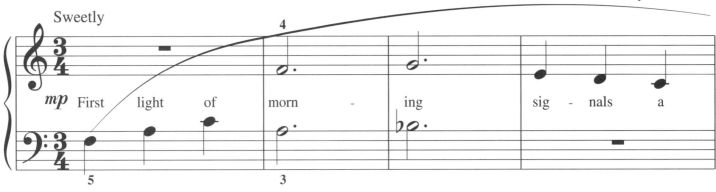

First light of morn - ing sig - nals a

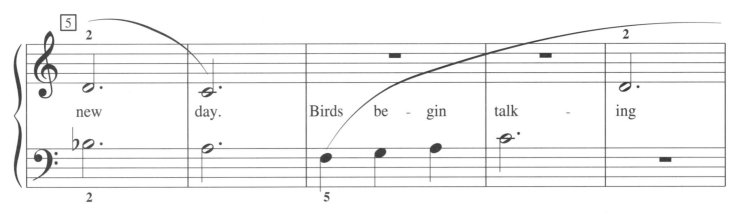

new day. Birds be - gin talk - ing

Accompaniment (Student plays one octave higher than written.) 🔊 **25/26**

Sweetly (♩=120)

28

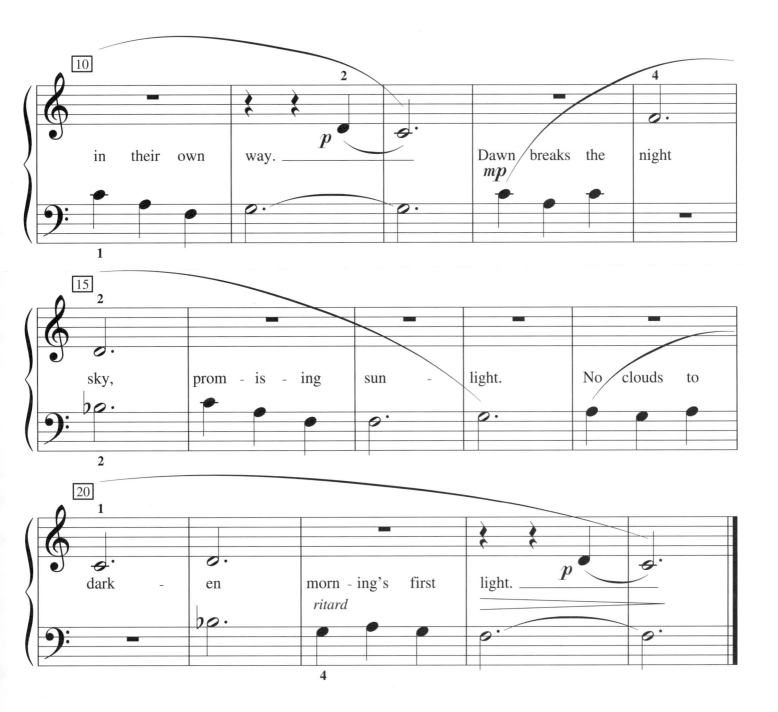

Ritard (*rit.*)

Circle the things that are slowing down little by little.

1. Play and sing the song below keeping a steady tempo.
2. Write a *rit.* sign in the blue box.
3. Play and sing the song again, gradually slowing the tempo in the last two measures.

Falling Asleep

Blink and nod is what I do be - fore I go to sleep.

Naturals

Trace the naturals below.

space natural   **line natural**

Draw a natural sign in the box before each note
and write the name of each note in the blank below it.

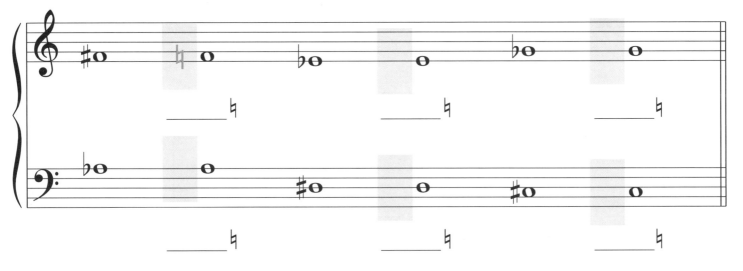

A sharp or flat lasts for one measure, unless a natural sign cancels it.
Write the correct answers below.

1. How many notes are played
as **F♯** in each measure?

2. How many notes are played
as **E♭** in each measure?

3. How many notes are played
as **B♭** in each measure?

4. How many notes are played
as **C♯** in each measure?

Grandmother's Lace

Flowing Waltz tempo

Carol Klose

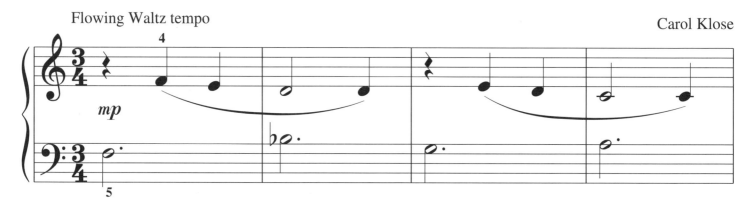

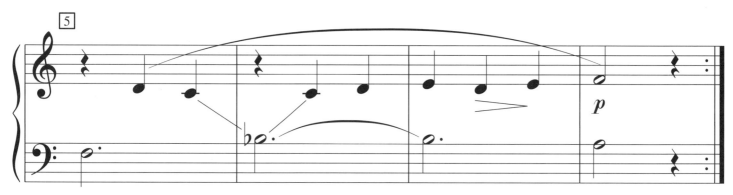

Accompaniment (Student plays one octave higher than written.) 🔊 **27/28**

Flowing Waltz tempo (♩ = 140)

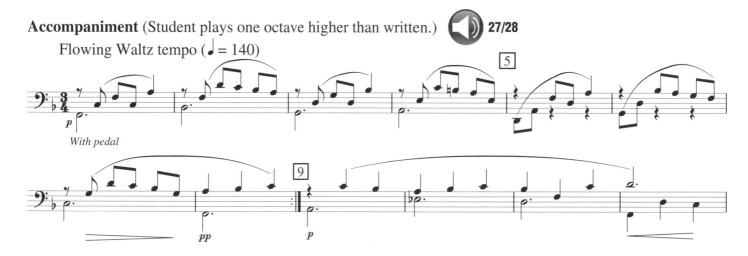

With pedal

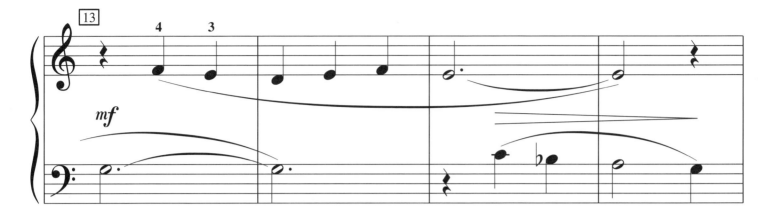

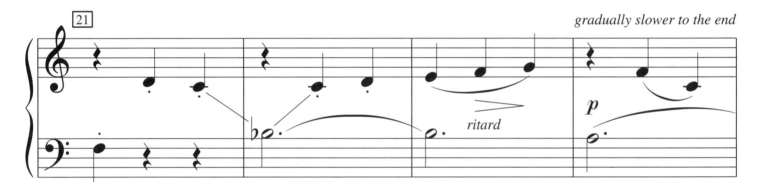

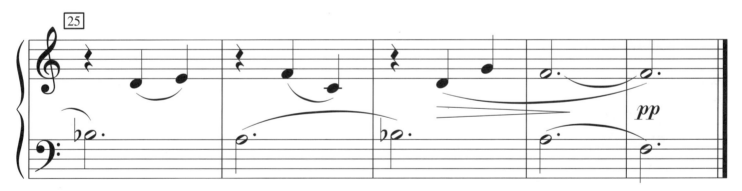

33

Inspector Hound
(Technique Tune)

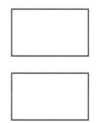
29/30

Make the two-note slurs sound "sneaky" by giving the first note of each slur more emphasis than the second. As you listen to *Inspector Hound*, play the two-note slurs in one arm movement.

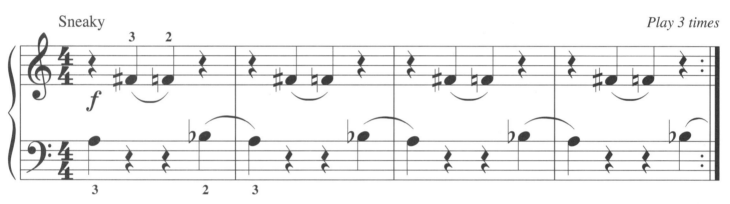

Sneaky   *Play 3 times*

Note: As a duet, the teacher plays "Inspector Hound" on page 35 8va higher and the student plays the Technique Tune 8va lower.

Read & Discover

Eye spy!

Using page 35 as a guide, write the answers to the following questions in the boxes below.

1. How many different pitches does the R.H. play?

2. How many different pitches does the L.H. play?

NATURAL

A **Natural** sign cancels a sharp or flat. Play the **Natural** (white) key.

Inspector Hound

29/30

Phillip Keveren

Lowest D
on the piano

Too Cool!

Slow Blues

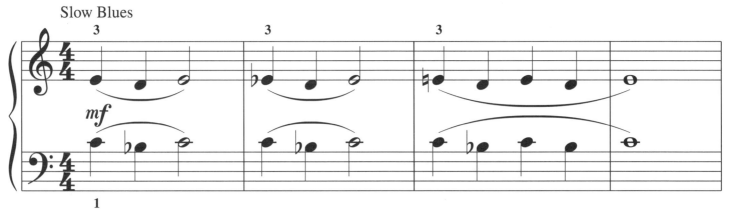

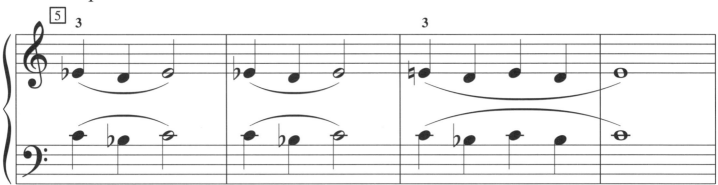

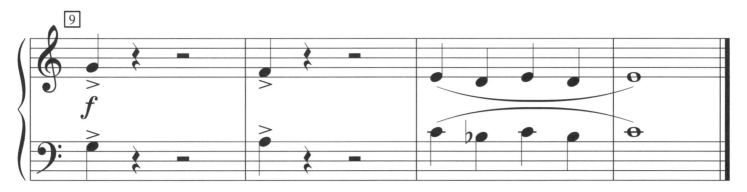

Accompaniment (Student plays one octave higher than written.) 31/32

Slow Blues (♪♪ = ♪ ♪)(♩=100)

36

Sign Quest

1. Write a sharp (♯) sign in front of all the **F's**.
2. Write a flat (♭) sign in front of all the **E's**.
3. Play the song and give it a title.

Title: _____

Those Creepy Crawly Things
On The Cellar Floor

Stepping very carefully (♩ = 140) 33/34

Carol Klose

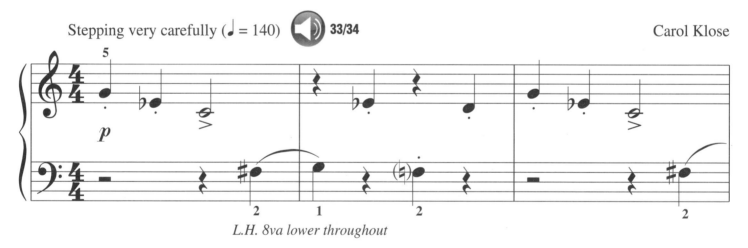

L.H. 8va lower throughout

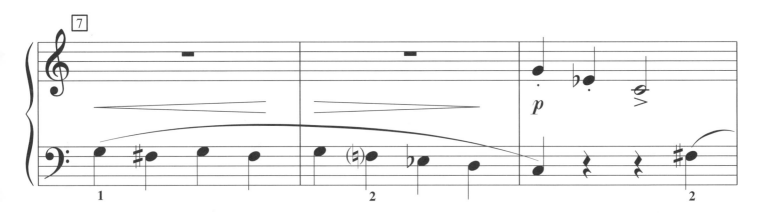

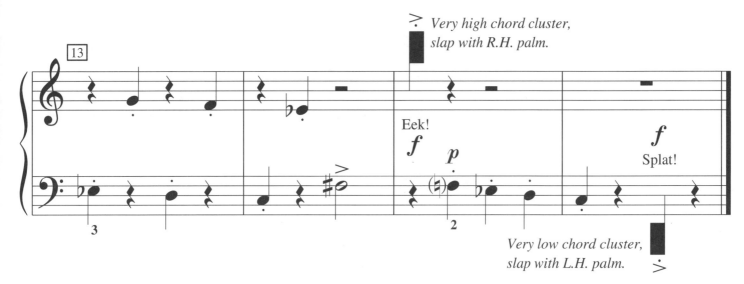

> Very high chord cluster,
> slap with R.H. palm.

Eek!

f   **p**

f

Splat!

Very low chord cluster,
slap with L.H. palm.

Symbol Road

Symbol Sam the Signpost Man is painting all the signs along Symbol Road. Complete the job by drawing the correct musical symbol for each signpost.

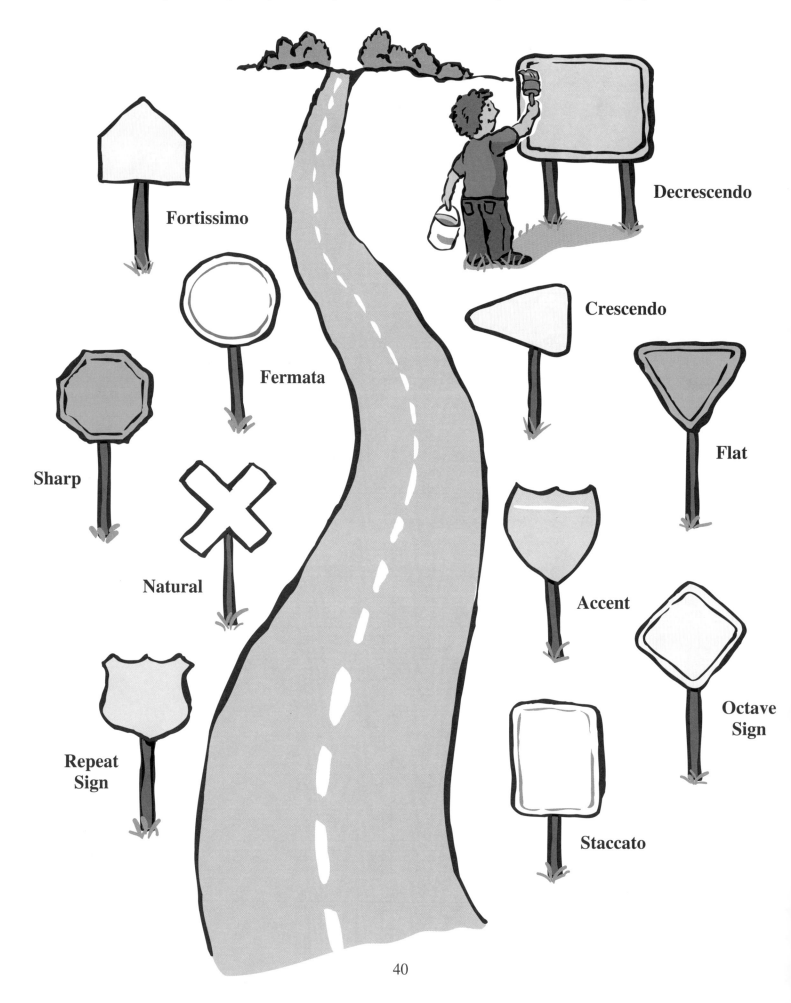

FERMATA

A **Fermata** means to hold a note longer than its rhythmic value.

Bayou Blues

 35/36

Phillip Keveren

Slow and bluesy (♩=110)

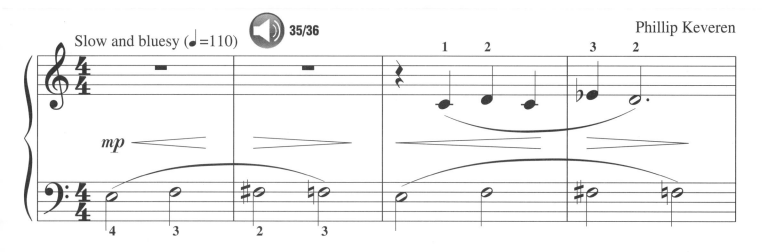

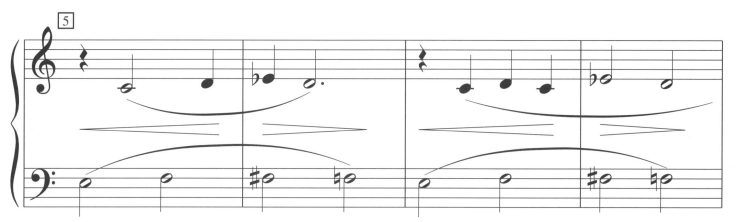

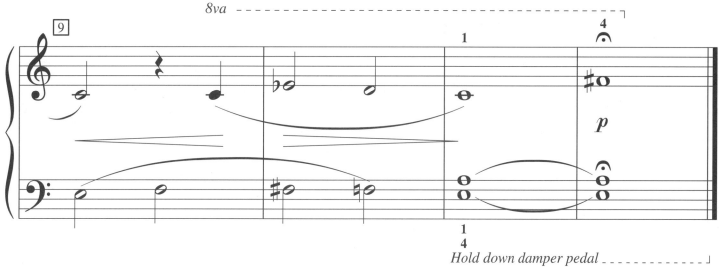

Hold down damper pedal

On Fourth Avenue

Leisurely, not fast (♩ = 120) 37/38

Fred Kern

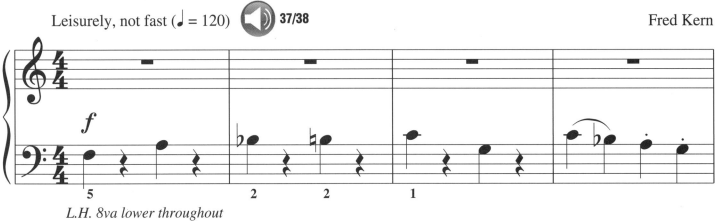

L.H. 8va lower throughout

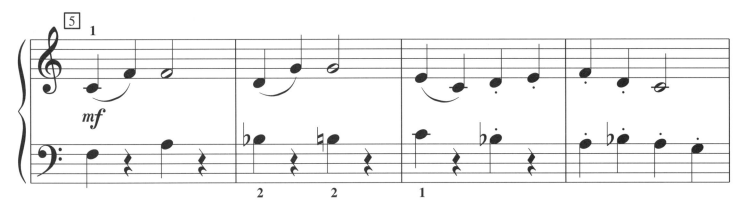

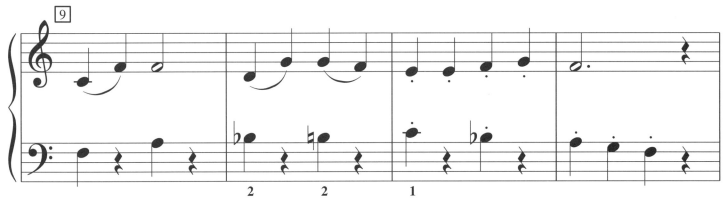

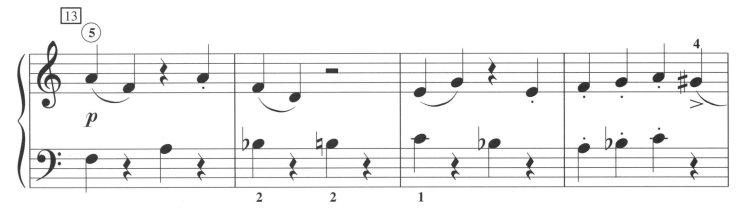

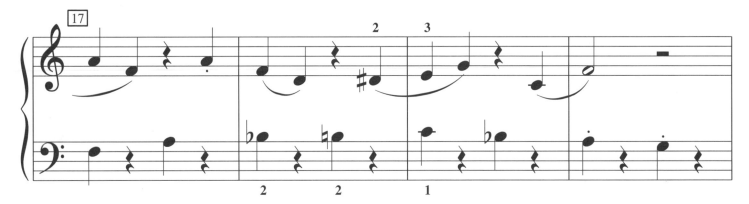

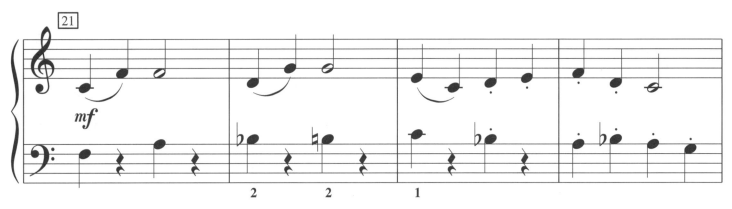

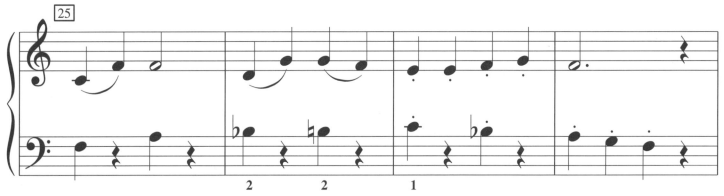

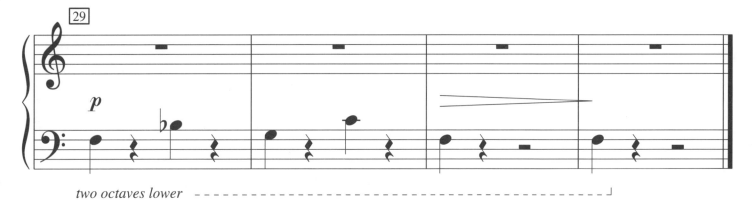

two octaves lower - ⌐

The Grand Staff – Playing On B C D

1. Write the names of the blank keys on the keyboard.
2. Trace the missing notes on the staff and draw a line to the correct key on the keyboard.

Complete the mystery tune below by drawing the missing quarter notes in the blue boxes. Play the piece and write its title.

Title: _____

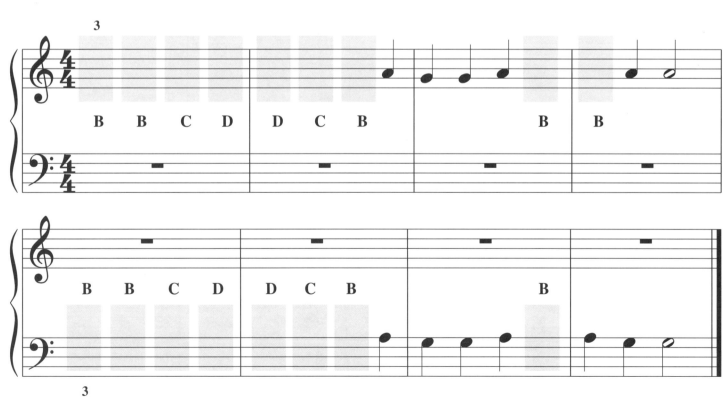

Ledger Lines

Party Cat is studying for a theory test.
Help him learn what ledger lines are by completing the sentence below.

1. Draw a ledger line D note in each blue box below.
2. Write the note names in the blanks below each note.

Lines ___ ___ ___ ___ ___

___ bov ___   or   ___ ___ low   the   st ___ ___ ___

are   ___ ___ lle ___   le ___ ger lines.

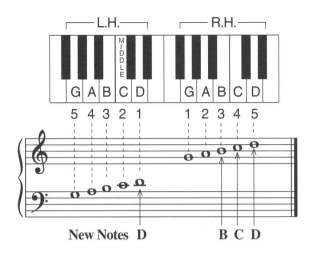

New Notes D   B C D

LEDGER LINES

Ledger Lines are added when notes are written higher or lower than the staff.

Summer Evenings

"Alouette"
Words by Barbara Kreader

Sweetly

mp Sum — mer   eve - nings,   moon - light through my   win — dow.

Star — light   shin - ing,   breez - es   blow - ing   sighs.

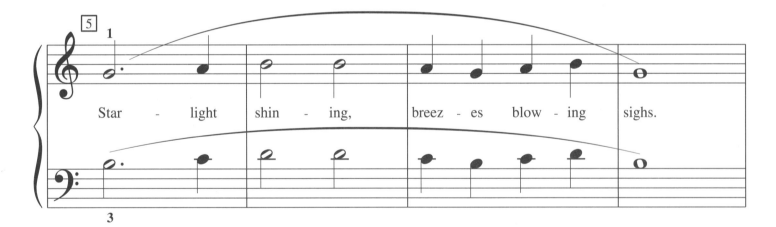

Accompaniment (Student plays one octave higher than written.) 🔊 **39/40**

Sweetly (♩=150)

p

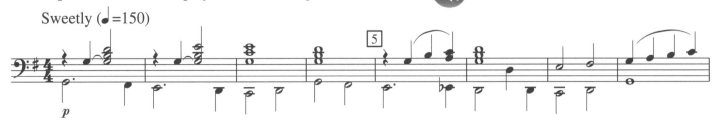

46

As I lie up - on my bed, sights and sounds soon fill my head.

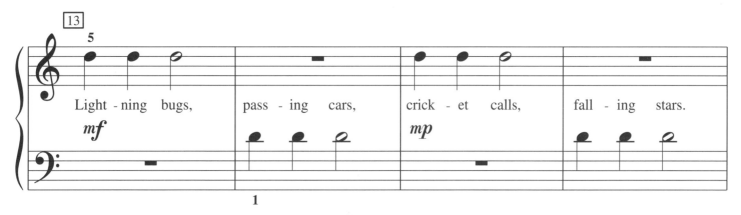

Light - ning bugs, pass - ing cars, crick - et calls, fall - ing stars.

mf *mp*

mf Sum - mer eve - nings warm and soft and still.

rit.

mp

p

mp

rit.

47

My Own Song
On G A B C D

Place both hands on G A B C D. Listen and feel the pulse as your teacher plays the accompaniment below.

With your right hand, play G A B C D. Experiment by playing D C B A G. Mix the letters any way you want and make up your own song!

With your left hand, play G A B C D. Experiment by playing D C B A G. Again, mix the letters any way you want and make up another song!

Have fun!

Accompaniment 🔊 41

Jazz Waltz (♩=170)

Repeat as necessary | *Last time*

Meet In The Middle

Accompaniment (Student plays one octave higher than written.) 🔊 **42/43**

Spike Is Puzzled!

Spike loves crossword puzzles.
Help him complete each word by writing the note names in the blanks.

Across

2. Houn___

4. P___rty

5. N___ws

10. ___in___o

11. Cir___l___

12. Do___

13. D___n___e

15. Son___

16. Qu___st

17. P___t

Down

1. ___ ___t

2. Ho___ ___own

3. ___et___ ___tive

6. Spik___

7. Ti___k

8. Tr___ ___s

9. Ji___

10. ___oun___e

14. Cl___p

Scattered Showers

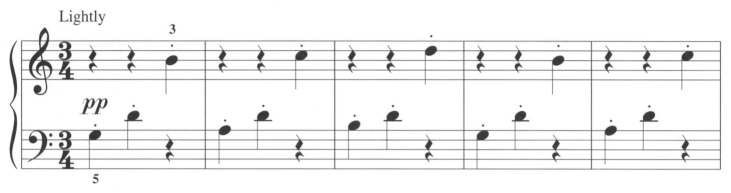

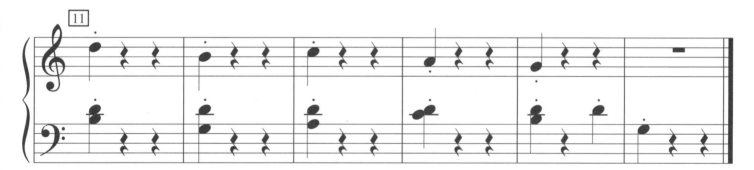

Accompaniment

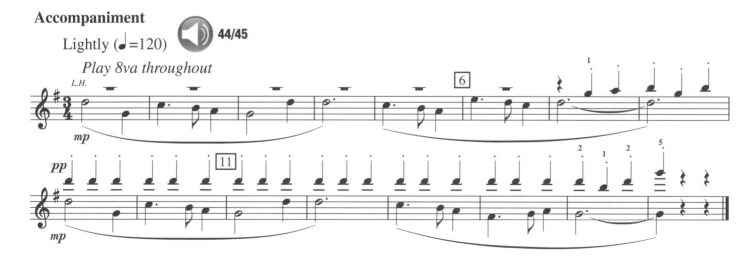

G A B C D Mysteries

1. Party Cat went shopping and lost his sunglasses.
   Complete the story below to find out what happened.

Party Cat left his sunglasses in a _____ when he was

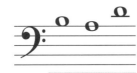 

riding in a _____ . We hope his _____

won't be mad at that _____ cat!

2. Bear has lost his music assignment. Where is it?

_____ e _____ r _____ roppe _____ his _____ ssi _____ nment

in Spike's foo _____ _____ owl _____ nd Spike _____ te it!

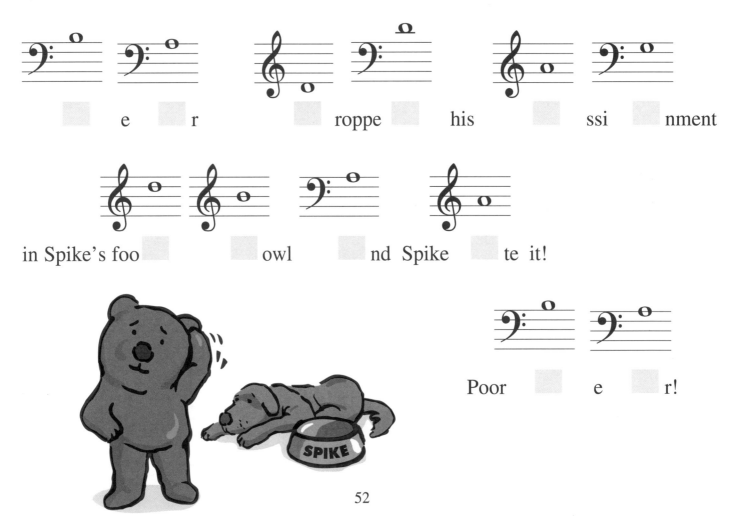

Poor _____ e _____ r!

52

Pop!

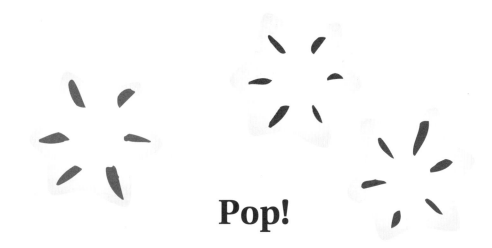

Bouncy (♩=200) 46/47

"Pop Goes The Weasel"

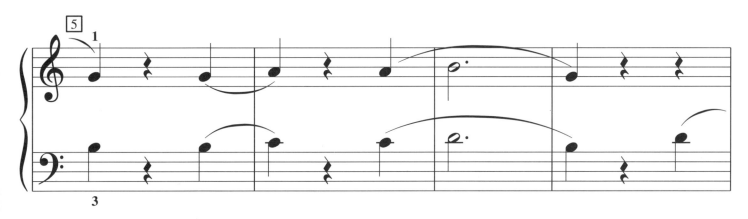

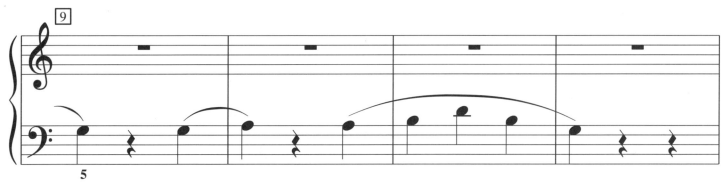

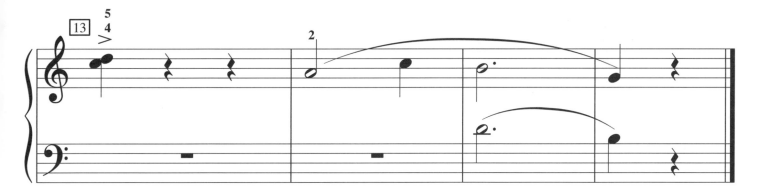

Imagine & Create

🔊 41

Pop!
(Activity Page)

Create a new piece in A B A form!

1. As you listen to the accompaniment to *My Own Song On G A B C D*, play *Pop!* (page 53) one octave higher than written. This is the A section of your piece.

A   Bouncy

mf   *Continue as written*

2. Using the notes G A B C D, make up your own B section by improvising for eight or more measures.

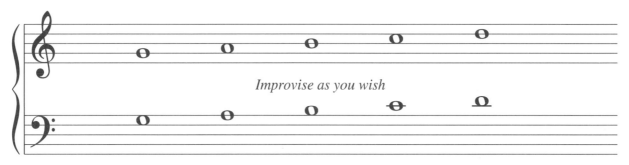

B

Improvise as you wish

3. Return to the beginning of *Pop!* (in jazz, that's called the "head") and play to the end of the piece.

A

mf   *Continue as written to end of song*

Octave Sign   *8va-¬*

Bear, Party Cat and Spike play in the band.

1. Play *Pop Goes The Weasel* and decide which instrument would play the high, the middle, and the low parts.
2. Write the name of the correct instruments in each blue box.

flute   trumpet   tuba

Bouncy

PIANISSIMO

pp

means very soft.

Go To Sleep

Andante

Folk Tune

Slum - ber time is draw - ing near, night - time gath - 'ring 'round us.
Stars will all be bright and clear when the sand - man finds us.

Dream sweet dreams the long night through. Moth - er will be near to you.

Go to sleep, my dear one. Go to sleep, my dear one.

Accompaniment (Student plays one octave higher than written.) 48/49

Andante (♩=110)

Dynamic Play

Party Cat is sneaking up on Spike.
Guide his footsteps by writing the dynamic marks
from softest to loudest in the boxes below.

Add music to this story by playing the notes next to each dynamic marking.

Goofy Gadget

Sputtering along steadily (♩ = 200)  **50/51**

Both hands 8va lower throughout

Phillip Keveren

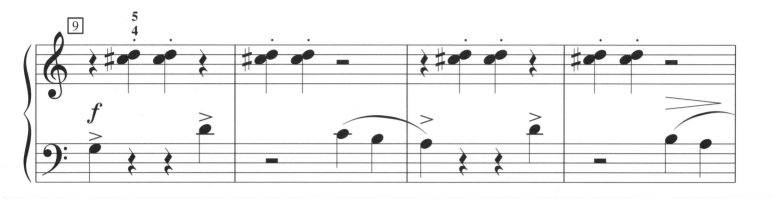

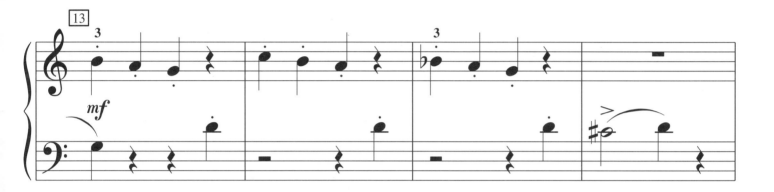

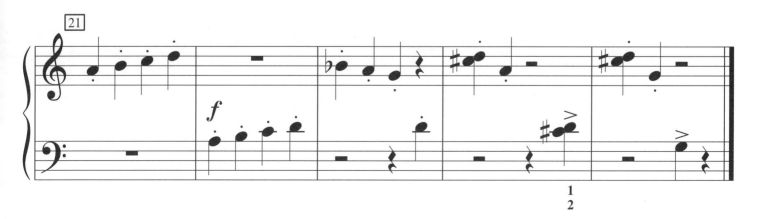

Upbeat

Help the leprechaun feel the upbeats.

1. Every example has two upbeats. First, trace the barline
   that separates the upbeats, then add barlines to complete
   each example. Because of the upbeat, the last measure
   will be incomplete.

2. Write the counts in the blanks and clap each example.

Jig

Lively (♩=210) 🔊 **52/53**

Irish

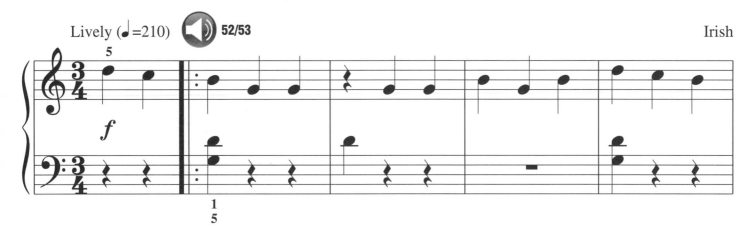

f

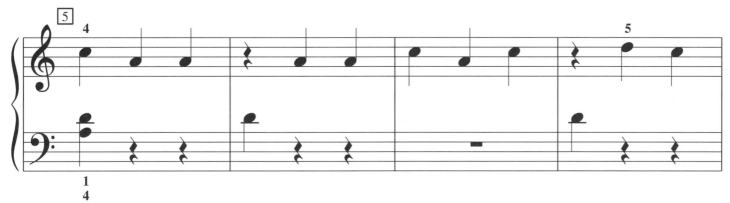

Play 1st time only. **Play 2nd time.**

1. 2.

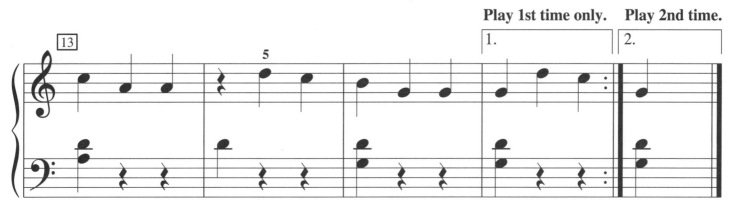

Rhythm Detective

Find the missing notes and rests!

1. Draw the missing note or rest in the blue boxes.
   Use each symbol from the detective's hat only once.
2. Clap and count each example.

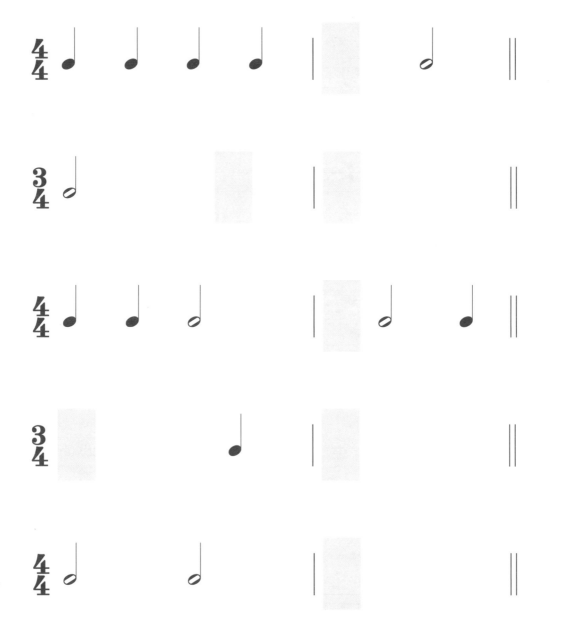

Interval Food

It's dinnertime and Spike is hungry.
Find out what he likes to eat.

Go to the keyboard and play each clue.
Write the name of the last key you land
on in the blue box.

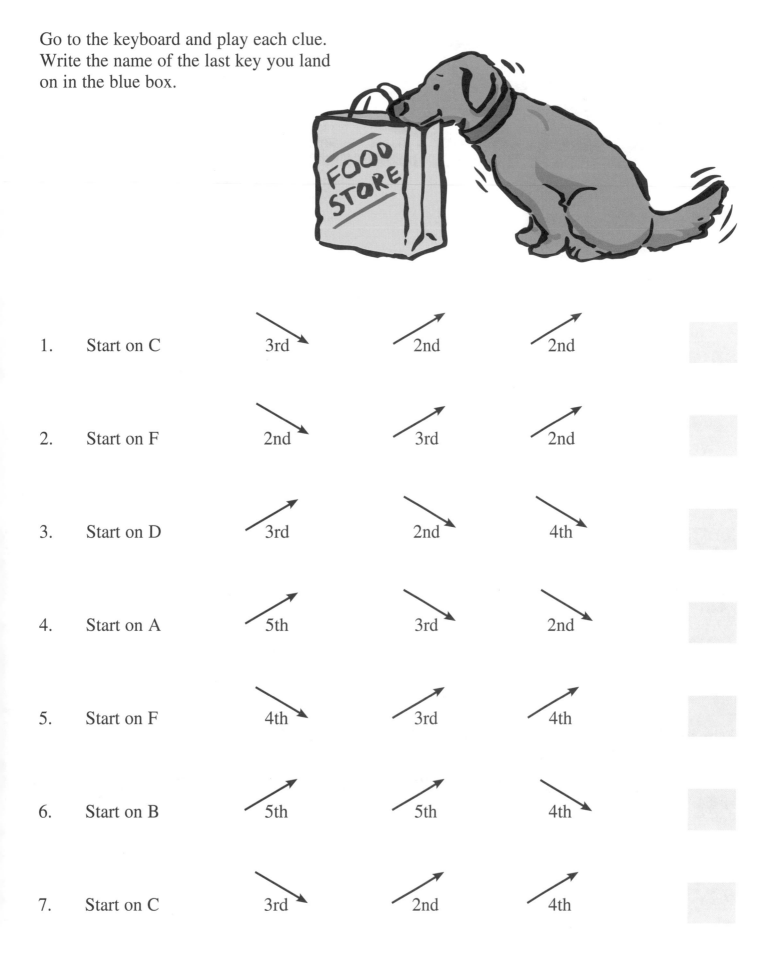

1. Start on C   3rd ↘   2nd ↗   2nd ↗

2. Start on F   2nd ↘   3rd ↗   2nd ↗

3. Start on D   3rd ↗   2nd ↘   4th ↘

4. Start on A   5th ↗   3rd ↘   2nd ↘

5. Start on F   4th ↘   3rd ↗   4th ↗

6. Start on B   5th ↗   5th ↗   4th ↘

7. Start on C   3rd ↘   2nd ↗   4th ↗

Go For The Gold

Stately March

Phillip Keveren

Accompaniment (Student plays one octave higher than written.) 🔊 **54/55**

Stately March (♩=90)

Go For The Gold

(Activity Page)

54/55

Join the *Go For The Gold* orchestra!

1. As you listen to the accompaniment to *Go For The Gold*, imitate the sound of the piccolo parts. Play the following piccolo parts two octaves higher than written.

2. As you listen to the accompaniment again, imitate the sound of the tuba. Play the following tuba part two octaves lower than written.

Interval Roundup

1. Using the arrows as your guide, draw whole notes to build the intervals on each staff.
2. Draw X's on the keys that match each interval.

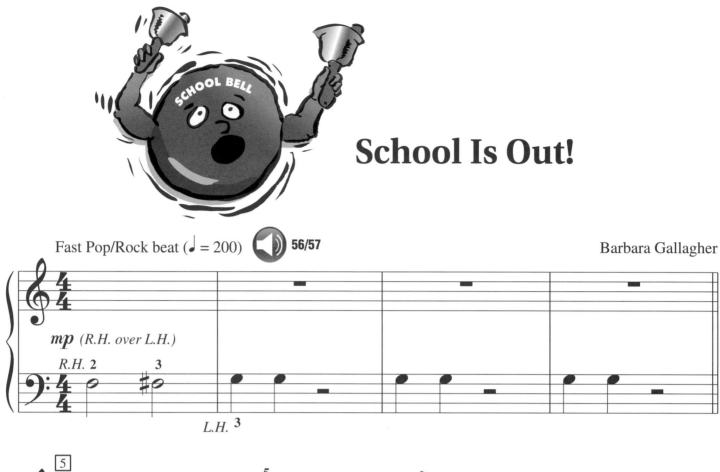

School Is Out!

Fast Pop/Rock beat (♩ = 200) 🔊 **56/57**

Barbara Gallagher

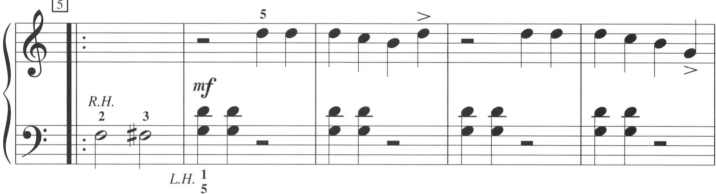

68

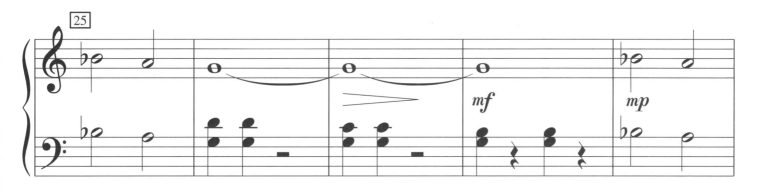

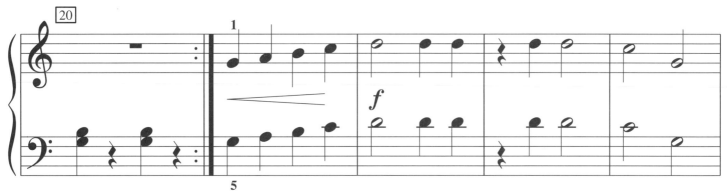

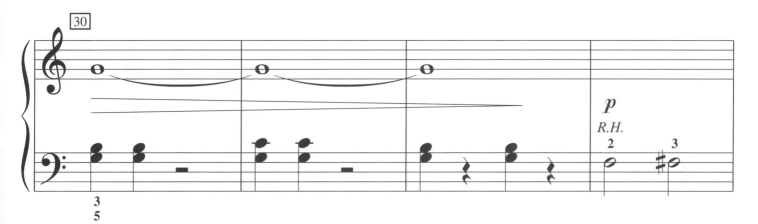

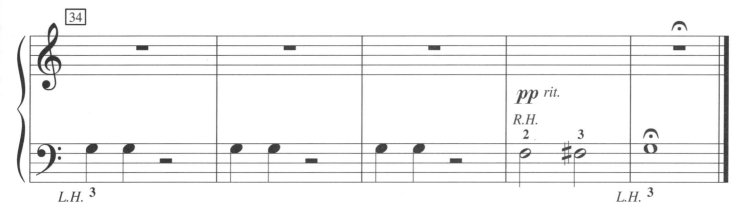

Relay Review

Spike and Party Cat are racing to finish their *All-In-One Piano Lessons Book D!*
Match the correct answers by drawing a line from Column A to Column B.
Record your time in the box at the end of each race.

START

A	B
(fermata symbol)	Bass C D E
(treble notes)	tie
(3/4 notes)	staccato
(bass notes)	fermata
(treble notes)	legato
(notes)	harmonic 2nd
(bass notes)	harmonic 3rd
(bass notes)	upbeat
(bass notes)	harmonic 4th
(treble notes)	melodic 4th
(bass notes)	accent

START

A	B
pp	slow tempo gradually
rit.	melodic 5th
(notes)	octave sign
♯	crescendo
(treble notes)	flat
(crescendo sign)	slur
(bass notes)	ledger line D
8va ----	pianissimo
♭	decrescendo
(decrescendo sign)	sharp
(bass notes)	harmonic 5th

The winner is:

_____

FINISH Seconds   **FINISH** Seconds

70

Teacher's Examples

Page 16 (Play)   1. Play all.
2. Play only the section indicated.

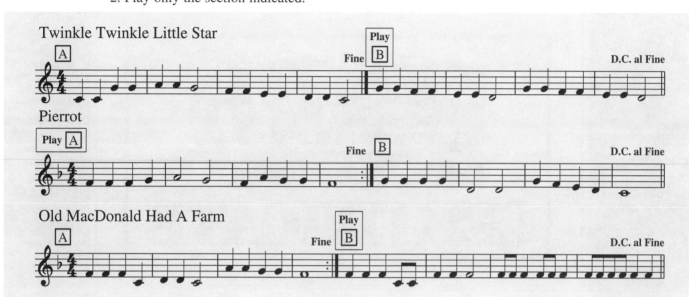

AWARD CERTIFICATE

_____

HAS SUCCESSFULLY COMPLETED
HAL LEONARD ALL-IN-ONE
PIANO LESSONS, BOOK D
AND
IS HEREBY PROMOTED TO
BOOK THREE.

_____   _____

TEACHER   DATE

HAL•LEONARD®